All About Love

This is a work of fiction. The events and characters described herein are imaginary and are not intended to refer to specific places or living persons. The opinions expressed in this manuscript are solely the opinions of the author and do not represent the opinions or thoughts of the publisher. The author has represented and warranted full ownership and/ or legal right to publish all the materials in this book.

Dedication

This book is dedicated to my grandson Henry. An avid reader at the precocious age of two but more importantly a great story teller. To my family, my wife Teri, daughter Christine and Son in law Jake, who at times actually tolerate my views no matter how far awry they tend to go. Lastly to my Brothers and Sisters in the Corp. who Inspired many of the works in this book.

There are many types of Love. Love is not all cards and flowers, holding hands, exchanging glances, kissing and feeling as if you could not go on if you were separated from that love or lover. Love of Country and Patriotism, is also love. Love of Friends and Brothers who have passed on who we Love and miss. There is Love of Family and Holidays spent with those people we cherish. There is also Love of Nature and of Life. These are all forms of Love which we carry with us and experience everyday. If Love fills the world then Hate cannot exist because Love is all consuming.

One of my favorite quotes comes from Marianne Williamson : *A Return to Love,* "Our deepest fear is not that we are inadequate. Our deepest fear is that we are powerful beyond measure. It is our light not our darkness that most frightens us. We ask ourselves who are we to be brilliant, gorgeous, talented, fabulous? Actually, who are we not to be? You are a child of God Your playing small does not serve the world. There is nothing enlightened about shrinking so that others will not feel insecure. We are all meant to shine as children do. " Go forth and shine brighter than the brightest star because you are that great.

Table Of Contents

Patriotic Love

Our Flag

The rain falls lightly there's a gentle breeze,
Our flag extends and falls with relative ease.
I cannot help the great sadness I feel,
As some arrogant people decided to kneel.

Forward info battle you inspire their cries,
Troops charge beneath you but so many die.
You cover their coffins as a nation cries,
Your arrogance continues its hateful rise.

This flag flies above you with ultimate pride,
To honor all those who gave all and died.
They sacrificed all they had, yet you deny.
How dare your hatred dishonor those lives.

I look to that flag and I love it with passion,
I don't care what you think or if it's in fashion.
One day long ago I swore an oath to defend it,
And as long as I breathe I will do all to defend it.

Old Glory

To some you are a piece of cloth easily discarded,
To others you are the symbol of everything regarded.
To me you are the symbol of all that I hold sacred,
For what you've done and where you've been the world should be elated.

You were there in the beginning as we struggled to be free.
You were there with Mr. Lincoln as he fought with Mr. Lee.
You were there with Teddy Roosevelt as he charged up San Juan Hill.
You were with them in the trenches and charging to the hills.

You saw new and deadlier weapons in a war to end all wars.
You were with us at Pearl Harbor and D Day to be sure.
You were with us at the Chosin in that short Korean War.
Then you came with us to Vietnam, it broke our hearts that war.

You traveled far to outer space and stand proudly on the moon,
Then six more times we planted you on return trips to the moon.
You flew proudly on the towers on the day they met their doom,
And you flew atop the rubble as we searched among the ruins.

Then you came along to the Middle East in a land of sun and sand.
You marched through many countries across that heated sand.
Through all of this you showed our pride everywhere you went.
You also covered all the souls of those who fell in death.

Through all the years and all the tears beside us all the way,
No matter where, no matter when you always led the way.
Tell me how one young or old could ignore this awesome debt.
To me, and mine, you're a sacred cloth and will be till my death.

Ghost of The Towers

Two beams of light a simple sight, of beauty and of grace,
Ascending to the heavens from this bloodied sacred place.
A ghost of the two towers whose beauty stands no more,
It marks a pile of rubble mixed with those who live no more.

The pain from this still haunts me so and will for evermore,
Eighteen years and tears still flow and fall upon the floor.
The terrible loss we suffered that day, cut me to the core,
Three thousand souls died that day and we've added many
more.

Yet today we remember all of them for just one single day,
Tomorrow we go back to life and to our passive ways.
It matters not how much we lost and how many had to pay,
Tomorrow we forget all of it, it's just another day.

I swore loudly on that day and I renew it here today,
I will not forget what was done in hate, nor will I forgive
that day.
As I look at the light, it's beauty and peace there's pain,
As Memories of 9-11 pierce my heart each and every day.

A Terrible Day

It's been eighteen years since that terrible day,
Some may say we've come a very long way.
Ground Zero is restored, a tower stands once more,
But the three thousand souls are among us no more.

We swore that day we would never forget,
Yet today we even ignore the eminent threat.
How could we have gone that far astray,
Forgetting the sacrifices made that day.

We remember the names we read them each year.
In a ceremony where we relive all our fears.
Yet the very next day we return to our lives,
Apologize to those who threaten our lives.

I remember my vow, I just cannot forget,
The price of three thousand souls I regret.
If you fail to remember and honor your vow,
We lost more that day than you really know.

Another Anniversary

Today the sun isn't going to shine,
Memories of sadness bring tears to my eyes.
I still see the planes against a clear blue sky,
Seconds away from taking their lives.

Three thousand souls we lost that day,
It seems like the pain will never go away.
I still pray to God each year on this day ,
Stretch out your hand, intervene some way.

Change the outcome and lessen the pain,
Too many souls have perished in vain.
Never have I felt pain like this before,
Shed many tears for those I knew not before.

Yet every year I live through it again,
Stark horrid images burned into my head.
One final prayer I utter this terrible day,
God hold them and love them especially today.

No One Could Predict

I made you a promise so long ago,
And to this day one thing I know
I carry it deep within my heart,
A hatred so deep it makes life dark.

I remember that day so very well,
No one could predict the arrival of hell.
At 8:46 am the first plane struck ,
Followed by the second as 9:03 struck.

Fire and smoke did fill the skies,
Some say Satan stood there and smiled.
Three thousand souls did die that day,
Never again to see the light of day.

The towers crashed as we all cried,
We sat and stared at the coverage live.
In anger and sorrow we swore out loud,
We will never forget what we allowed.

Now many years have passed and gone,
The snowflakes have forgotten long.
Thousands who died not important to them,
Passivity the reason it won't happen again.

But I promise you here on this very day,
I'll never back down, I'll never give way.
I made a promise a vow that sad day,
And I'll honor that vow till my dying day.

That Sacred Day

The day approaches in thunderous silence,
The pain, the tears, the horrendous violence.
This year will marks fifteen years of sorrow,
When three thousand souls had no tomorrow.

We promised, we vowed, we swore in anger,
That we would not forget our sorrow and anger.
But some must have mellowed or dismayed,
Because all these brave souls have been betrayed.

Today a mosque defiles the soil of ground zero,
Soil still containing the blood of so many heroes.
It makes me so incredibly sad to remember this,
That a once great nation could fall low to this.

We made promises that day in oceans of tears,
How could they mean nothing in the coming years.
That day of infamy that day of ultimate sadness,
Lives on in my heart as the ultimate of sadness.

On that sacred day, on a beautiful September morn,
Took a piece of my heart causing me to mourn.
If that piece of my heart could have saved only one
I would have given more gladly to save everyone.

Homeless

The nights are colder the air is crisp,
We retreat to our houses a fire is lit.
Not all of us have this I'm sorry to say,
Many vets are homeless with no place to stay.

They fought wherever we sent them to,
Fighting for freedom and red white and blue.
These are our finest the best of our land,
Bravely they fought in jungle and sand.

Coming home some were wounded,
But some wounds can't be seen.
Dark dreams ravaged their minds to bring them to tears,
As death and devastation made them relive their fears..

The nation who sent them offered no help,
People they defended were blind to results.
They wander our streets an army once proud,
Suffering in silence as they keep underground.

Before we worry about those of other lands,
Before political fund raisers get out of hand.
Give thought to that soldier, sailor or Marine,
All of these veterans who had many dreams.

We owe them so much we can never repay,
Not just the nation, but all us too should pay.
Not just with change or a few dollar bills.
But respect and acknowledgement of all that is due.

Lost

I saw a man in the street today,
His face unshaven beard of gray.
His jacket once in battle worn,
Tattered, torn and no longer warm.

On his tattered coat of green he wore,
A ribbon and a medal of times before.
The medal he wore was a Navy Cross,
The man was a hero but now is lost.

How can we not see this terrible wrong,
One of our heroes suffering hard and long.
He's there before us day and night,
We look right past him as if he's not in sight.

He was a hero one of our nations best,
He stood tall for us once above all the rest.
If he stood for us can we not stand for him,
Give him what a nation once promised him.

When I think of him it makes me very sad,
A nations hero that we would treat so bad.
Have we not lost enough at war through death,
That we may lose another in a single breath.

Remember what he's given for us all,
As we walk by not seeing him at all.
So won't you stop and pay homage as is due,
To a Nations Hero who gave all for you.

Memorial Day

From Gettysburg to Arlington,
Ardennes and Flanders Field.
Our heroes lie in eternal rest,
Beneath Crosses, Stars or Stones.

They lost their lives in battle,
So that we could all be free.
So on this day we bow our heads,
And respectfully make this plea.

Dear God please take a moment,
To embrace our fallen veterans.
We honor the sacrifices they made,
When they gave up all their tomorrow's.

So before you go and celebrate,
Honor this simple request.
Bow your head and say a prayer,
You're praying for the best.

Remember

On this year's Memorial Day,
As I contemplate our great losses.
I wish I had something great to say,
But instead I can only humbly Pray.

May I be worthy of the gift you gave me,
May I treasure it through all my days.
May I remember others may need to follow,
In those large footprints you have blazed.

May I be ready when my turn comes near,
Fight as fierce as you without any fear.
The price of freedom is very, very dear,
And I will defend it throughout, all my years.

A Hero's Bones

As I walk past rows of markers and flags,
My mind wanders as my gait slows and drags.
I read the names upon the cold grey stones,
Knowing buried below are a hero's bones.

The date on the stones tell a story of war,
Where many brave warriors fell by scores.
They sacrificed all till there was no more,
Ensuring our freedom remains forevermore.

To the heroes who no longer fight the war,
Who lie at rest and are among us no more.
We remember and honor you on this day ,
So all will know your sacrifice was not in vain.

Freedom Takes a Terrible Toll

In so many lands across the seas,
Thousands of crosses can be seen.
They line the land in perfect rows,
To mark the graves of fallen souls.

Souls that fell in many battles great,
History records their names by date.
We remember them all on this date,
As we offer up our prayers and praise.

Each year this day we honor those,
Each year we find their number grows.
The price of freedom takes a terrible toll,
We give thanks to God for these brave souls

One Last Time

If I should die suddenly in the night,
Stumbling here and losing my fight.
I want the world I leave here behind,
To know of my love I leave behind.

It started long ago as a little boy,
Playing in battles with guns as toys.
That flag would take my breath away,
As that beautiful music began to play.

More beautiful than sung by a heavenly host,
I remember distinctly as I cried there the most.
God let me touch it for just one more time,
It matters not the color red or white will be fine.

The square of blue showing peace for us all,
The stars shinning brightly to honor us all.
Remember I loved her in good and bad times,
She loved me back as she covered me that last time.

Lives Interrupted

On this Memorial Day I silently reflect,
As I pass the cold gray markers set
Of my brothers and sisters who lie at rest,
Having served this country with their best.

At different times and in many different wars,
To defend our freedom from shore to shore.
Some fell in battles too many to name,
Some came home but we're never the same.

To many this day is about the start of summer,
But the real purpose was clearly another.
This is the day we set aside to honor those,
Who gave so much defending against our foes.

Lives interrupted and put on hold,
Lives lost lie in the ground so cold.
Brothers and sisters side by side,
Protecting us from the darker side.

So on this day of peace and honor,
Remember those who showed this honor.
Stop a moment take the time to remember,
The freedom we enjoy today we owe to another.

Celebrate Our Memories

Happy Birthday to my beloved Corps,
Who changed my life forevermore.
You filled my boyish heart with pride,
You challenged me until I cried.

Upon yellow footprints I did land,
Where heroes did before me stand.
And although a hero I was not,
I learned to be a Marine was quite a lot.

To me there is a code to live by,
Honor, Corps, God and Country.
All of these you had me learn,
As my sacred symbol I did earn.

To you I owe so very, very much,
My love and loyalty seems not enough.
So on this 242nd year of your birth,
I join brothers and sisters and celebrate.

Many Years Ago

Many years ago I stood upon some footprints,
All that I am today are traced to those footprints.
A cold, scared little boy unsure about his future,
Is the man you see today in charge of that future.

I have travelled long and far these many years,
A life filled with pride not knowing any fear.
Yet times have changed since those great days,
A once great nation has fallen on bad days.

It no longer shows love for all who once served,
Instead illegals and refugees claim our reserves.
Our veterans are homeless and cold in the street,
Tears cover my face more as I can feel the defeat.

Our warrior heroes come home broken and torn,
Our nation seems heartless to Americas born.
Maybe we went wrong on our life's long journey,
When it didn't matter if our leaders were military.

How can this nation once great and successful,
Treat all of our veterans and elders so disgraceful.
Those to whom this nation has shown support,
Disrespect our nations flag and spit on our laws.

Today we need leaders like the ones we once had,
That lifted our nation from the scumbags and hags
So suck up your fears and stand tall in the pack,
Your fights not yet over bring your bad ass back.

Iwo Jima

They landed on the island of volcanic ash,
Fighting for hours to move only a dash.
Twenty thousand Japanese dug in to stay,
Kept the Marines from advancing that day.

Marines never quit, never stop or retreat,
They kept shelling and moving if only feet.
Five long days the battle did rage uphill,
Till they reached the top of that Suribachi hill.

Reaching the top the colors were raised,
A photo was taken that instilled praise.
An image that lives in History and Lore,
The image of the United States Marine Corps.

Witness

You've flown so proudly since it all began,
A brand new nation and a brand new land.
Carried into battles here and foreign lands,
Covering the caskets of every fallen man.

Created for a nation yearning to be free,
Carried by an army so all people could be free.
Carried across the seas for a war to end all wars,
Returning there once again to fight a second war.

Carried then to South Korea, at Chosin to be sure,
Then on again to Vietnam a most unpopular war.
Shedding tears along with us, as the towers fell,
Flying high in Arab lands, the blazing sands of hell.

Folded on the mantel in memory of a loved one,
One who gave it all, to guarantee our freedom.
Draped upon the coffins of all our fallen heroes,
Today waving in the breeze by the markers of the fallen.

Today you serve as witness to honor all the fallen,
Those who gave it all, in the battles that you led us
They won't be at the picnic, you will not hear their voice,
On this day remember them, and everything they gave.

Wake Up America

Wake up America this is really so wrong,
These are your children Americas first born.
They answered your call to come and give aid,
They picked up a weapon and joined the brigade.

They selflessly gave forsaking all that they had,
Fighting in battles where their brothers fell dead.
Coming home to a nation unwelcome by most,
Suffering from wounds unseen like a ghost.

These are the bravest giving all that they had,
Is it too much to ask that we give them a bed.
Look at them now as you walk on your way,
Then ask how can a nation treat them this way.

I Love This Great Flag

My precious flag has flown over many lands,
Has seen many battles at sea and on land.
Beneath it many brave patriots have fallen,
Their blood has baptized our flag and our land.

She leads us in battle in victory and defeat,
Old glory above us we cannot know defeat.
She marks times of sadness by flying low,
She covers our fallen at graveside below.

I love this great flag as it waves high above,
Because of the many who fell, spilling blood.
May God shine his grace on our great flag,
As he embraces those who fell for that flag.

Pride

As I walk through my many paths of life,
My legs and walk show the strain of life.
I shuffle, I limp and lean forward, as I walk,
It's nothing like when I walked the walk.

Every now and then as I'm shuffling along,
I hear a loud voice in the distance say.
Hey Marine, Semper Fi and I respond likewise,
As I walk I straighten up, my legs pick up the pace.

My step is quick, there's bounce again,
I'm marching at a pace like i did back then.
It happens each time I here those words,
Semper Fi Marine, still instills great pride.

Birthday Wishes

Here's to you, and you and you my friend,
And each one of my brothers and sisters.
Fill your glasses and hoist them high,
As we share a toast loudly Semper Fi.

From the day we stood the footprints,
Till we lie flat and still in the ground.
You are all my brothers and sisters,
Of each one of you I am really proud.

Today we celebrate our birthday,
As we share our bond together.
Remember this for all your days,
We stand tall and proud forever.

Walk With Me

Walk with me my brother and see the land we served,
The Stars and Stripes fly high above but not for all deserved.
We fail our veterans everyday not giving what there due,
And seniors shortchanged every year so others get what's due.

We are a land of immigrants who came here from afar,
And as each group did settle it they learned and followed law.
They learned and spoke our language and worked for all their needs,
Unlike those who come today and expect for all their needs.

They stood for our glad each day and pledged allegiance too,
They fought and died side by side Irish German and Jew.
The only color or race we saw was the one of red white and blue,
Today the come and do not stand nor give our flag it's due.

Instead they burn our flag in hate of everything we are,
They stand on it bringing us to tears as they desecrate our soul.
With no respect but just contempt they demand what isn't due,
To this I say go far from here we defend our flag from you.

Romantic Love

An Unforgettable Night

A very dark night as the waves crashed ashore,
It was an unforgettable night with the one I adored.
Staggering together in shifting sands beneath us,
Embracing each other sharing a kiss between us.

Observing the horizon where the moon met the sea,
Arm in arm observing a view so magnificent to see.
The color the reflection a true lovers scheme,
Only God himself could create such a scene

A scene from a fairytale for two lovers to enjoy,
Two lovers couldn't ask for or seek anymore joy.
The way the moon shines and touches the sea,
The sea appears as glass as far as one can see.

Two lovers embrace and step onto the glass,
Dancing to and fro as their shadows are cast.
Their silhouette shown on the moon so bright,
All through eternity I will remember this night.

A Walk Down Memory Lane

Yet another walk down memory lane,
It's forever changing and never the same.
Will I fixate on the many Happy Times,
Or lament the love lost that once was mine.

A moonlit beach and a starry, starry sky,
A midnight walk causes tears in my eyes.
In my mind I hope beyond all that I know,
That when you get to heaven this will be so.

That I live with love and the happiest of thoughts,
In a time with no beginning no end of sorts.
Where hugs could last a thousand years,
A kiss be eternal rather than measured in years.

A Beautiful Sight

The moon sits high in the sky this night,
A beautiful sight and a wonderful light.
Shinning on lovers on this happy night,
Lighting the path that they travel this night.

As a lover who enjoys walks hand in hand,
We stagger and sway in the shifting sand.
Stopping to hold one another cheek to cheek,
Whispering in your ear of my love you seek.

Beneath the light I pledge you my love,
You're more important than the stars above.
I look at the footprints we left in the sand,
They tell a story of two lovers in the sand

Open Arms

I stand before you with open arms,
Welcoming you with boyish charm.
I want to protect you from all harm,
Come to me inside my open arms.

Have no fear I will keep you safe,
My love surrounds you in this place.
Showering kisses to ease your fears,
My hands soothingly wipe your tears.

Embraced by love in its purest form,
Safe from the world as a mothers newborn.
I give you this and take nothing away,
As I wish you here would forever stay.

The Poet

Has the poet lost the words to write,
The words that tell of love and life.
The nouns and verbs that come to life,
Telling the tales of love and strife.

Words describing the stars so bright,
Moonlit sands on an enchanted night.
Lovers walking beneath the light,
Making promises in the dark of night.

Chivalrous knights on steeds of white,
Rescuing maidens from the evils of life.
Riding the lands in armor so bright,
Banners of color dancing in the light.

Please dear poet find the words to write,
Tell us now of the great loves of life.
Make us feel that cherished glow,
Of happiness that only lovers know.

My Eyes Betray Me

Sometimes my eyes betray me as the tears begin to flow,
I think of how I love you and the life I want to know.
I hold your hand and kiss your lips dreaming life away,
I tightly hold you in my arms you take my breath away.

It's so easy to say I love you they are words upon a page,
But the love I feel for you today has set my heart ablaze.
You are my waking moment as I rise before the sun,
And you are the last thing I think of when the day is done.

As we travel to the future counting days off one by one,
My love for you does grow each day surpassing everyone.
As the tears flow I make this promise and seal it with a
kiss,
On this night I hold you dear from now until our death.

Kisses

I kiss your fingers one by one,
On each digit I express eternal love.
I turn your hand and kiss your palm,
Your true example of feminine charm.

I place a tender kiss upon each eye.
As I taste the tears shed from those eyes.
With each kiss I pray to seal your tears,
That from this day forward your tears will end.

Now to your lips I beg your love,
If it takes the help of God above.
With each kiss I steal I pray for love.
With each kiss I bestow I seal that love

Each Day

If you should ever fall in love again,
Remember us remember when.
The nights we shared without any sleep,
The promises we always meant to keep.

The times we met here face to face,
We held each other in loving grace.
Our eyes did lock in loves embrace,
Your lips so sweet I long to taste.

Each day we had a memory now,
Each day I live I pray and I vow.
To hold these memories close to me,
In hopes someday that I reunite with thee.

Sometimes I think that when we die,
We lie in peace but in our minds,
A memory plays to pass away the time,
I pray that memory is about our time.

My Soul

On this dark and starless night,
I send my soul on a lonesome flight.
To search for something I once lost,
A loss for which I pay a terrible cost.

My journey pains me through the night,
Memories of love, and a beautiful life.
I search the dark for those happy times,
Times we talked as the moon did shine.

Times we shared in our secret world,
Oh how I long for that wonderful world.
A long ride in the rain to a picnic lunch,
Rose petals on a bed a loving touch.

But every dawn when my soul returns,
Empty and hollow having failed to learn.
Where your heart is hidden and kept,
Means another night I have lost and wept.

A Most Beautiful Woman

In the years of my misspent youth,
I fell in love with one so cute.
A beautiful women stole my heart,
But eventually we were forced apart.

Memories of those great days prevail,
Drives and meeting make me smile.
A walk along the beach in the night,
Wind in our hair in the dark of night.

Meeting by a tree across from the store,
Off to the drive in apartment and more.
Our stolen moments we covet and share,
Myself and the beauty I loved and adored.

Serious and funny we shared it all,
Stealing a weekend with foam and all.
These are the memories I hold so dear ,
Of the most beautiful women I ever lost.

Welcome Darkness

Welcome darkness my good friend,
In you there's solace through the end.
In you my pain doesn't feel as great,
Your isolation protects me from my fate.

In you there's nothing here but dreams,
I sleep and dream to escape the screams.
The screams of silence and of despair.
An emptiness and loneliness everywhere.

What I treasured once exists no more
But in your darkness I can still explore.
What once I shared and did adore,
And now has left me and is no more.

Our Youth

Remember long ago our youth,
When we always spoke the truth.
Always said what's on our mind,
Never thought about the time.

Things seemed simple then,
Living life and fun with friends.
Never thought the days would end,
But now it seems it was all pretend.

I long for those days of carefree life,
Happiness and free from strife.
Dreams and plans so fresh and new,
From minds of those without a clue.

But today our lives are very real,
The sorrows in them we really feel.
The happiness we felt back then,
Is only a shadow of bygone when.

In The Shadows

I live in a world which is not dark nor light,
It's the one we see in morning and night.
When night is fading but before sunrise,
And after the sun sets but before moonrise.

This mythical time of shadows and grays,
Where memories and dreams deserted lay.
Abandoned here without future or hope,
By the masses of lovers unable to cope.

I move among them seeking mine to revive.
I know that I must do this to feel alive.
Life without dreams is too sad to think of,
Without dreams there's no hope to speak of.

So here I wander and search for mine,
We were separated by troubled times.
I must find it and revive it I can't let it die,
With it I am filled with such love and pride.

It's a dream of love and of happy times,
Where two lovers live with no regard for time.
I will find it I know it stands out from the rest,
It beats with the love I feel when we connect.

Alone

I look into your eyes so deep,
My heart excited skips a beat.
My hand so gently rubs your cheek,
Your skin so soft it makes me weak.

We stand together face to face,
Holding each other in loves embrace.
All at once the clocks strikes twelve,
Our lips connect and kiss at the bell.

The old year goes another comes in,
We know not what the new brings in.
When my eyes open I become aware,
I am standing alone you were never here.

I Am

I am the wind moving the wind chimes on a stormy night,
I am the noise that startles you as you walk home at night.
I am the shadow that catches your attention and then is gone.
I am the scent you smell that reminds you of me when gone.

I am the darkness that seems to dominate the night sky.
I am the starlight that guides you through your endless stride.
I am the courage you feel as you walk through the night.
I am the feeling that someone is with you as you navigate life.

I am the love I have for you and I am always with you.
My love takes on many forms to protect and watch over you.
I will always be with you to keep you safe, a shadow that follows,
Because I love you for always yesterday today and forever.

The Universe

The universe is vast and wide,
And we tell ourselves little lies.
We look to it as the home of God,
And Believe that heaven lies inside.

We wish and pray upon the stars,
Lovers embrace both near and far.
We pledge our love beneath the moon,
We dance by its light we kiss and swoon.

Then we think that when we die,
Our spirits will occupy the sky.
Our souls will rise into heavens domain,
To become a bright light on heavens plane.

Snowflakes

The snow falls lightly from the sky,
Each flake a tear that I have cried.
I miss you so since we've been apart,
And sadness fills my broken heart.

With you I learned so many things,
I learned the joys that love could bring.
The simple things two lovers share,
While holding hands and facing stares.

The snowflakes show my many tears,
It shows my sorrows and my fears.
But then they melt and go away,
And no one know my sadness stays.

Love of Departed Friends

A Message

Where I go now you cannot follow,
Please don't lament in tears and sorrow.
We will be together again someday,
As we are all a part of this eternal play.

You are not alone I'll be here with you,
Just in a different way than what we knew.
I am the wind that runs through your hair,
The sun that embraces you with loving care.

If you speak to me, I will listen,
I will answer you but you'll need to listen.
Think of me not that my life has ended,
Rather think of it as my journey is extended.

As You Lie In State

I stand before you as you lie in state,
Our nations flag above you draped.
I know not how you met your fate,
But here I stand to take your place.

I cannot take your place in battle,
I would if they would let me shuffle.
I will stand here and speak for you,
And tell all who listen the legend of you.

From my eyes fall the tears you never wept,
I will try to keep your promises unkept.
I stand for you as you would for me,
Brothers for eternity we will always be.

Honors

I stand in a cemetery cold and wet,
A stark open grave awaits a vet.
I know not this vet, except by name,
My duty, to pay honors to his remains.

My rifle cold through thin white gloves,
My mind speaks silently to God above.
The hearse arrives the time has come,
The detail smartly to attention comes.

A flag draped coffin is carried and placed,
Family and friends all sit with sullen face.
The speaker softly tells of a life well spent,
I think of the time in service this brother spent.

The command rings out so crisp and clear,
Port arms, half right, unlock, and prepare.
The time is here my cold hands grip the stock,
Ready, aim, fire, three successive shots.

Present Arms as the bugler plays farewell,
It wails and cries as solemnly we dwell.
Fold the flag with honor, care, as well as love,
God grant you rest, your missions done,

My Brother

My brother did depart this day,
His soul was freed and flew away.
High beyond the stars and moon,
To make his home in Brigadoon.

He's free of pain and troubles too,
Some may say he is better too.
But all of us will miss his boyish charm,
His laugh and smile and spin of yarn

Life of the party and friend to all,
Could turn a boring time to fun for all.
I miss you brother here and now,
You leave a void inside me now.

I know not what the future will bring,
Hope for a heaven seems very thin.
I hope I can find you in time and space,
Until then I love you and miss each day.

I Must Stay

The sun is bright the birds do sing,
On this day they don't mean a thing.
My brothers gone three days have past,
Today his body to the flames is cast.

I sit before you staring into empty space,
As sad as I am this is a peaceful place.
I have memories of us spending more time,
Flashbacks of a much happier time.

Now you go and I must stay behind,
The fates and Gods are so unkind.
I think of all the time wasted and lost,
The separation between us really cost

I always loved you and kept you in mind,
Your laughter charm and impish kind.
I miss you so much there is a hole in my heart,
From the piece taken with you as you depart.

A Land Beyond The Stars

There is a land beyond the stars,
Left at Jupiter and right at Mars.
A land where all our journeys end,
A place where dreams never end.

We'll reunite with who we love,
And celebrate our unclaimed love.
We'll live our dreams of happiness,
Without any guilt or sin to confess.

Eternity is ours, to love one another,
Holding, kissing, embracing each other.
Our kisses will last a thousand years,
Smiles and joy will replace all fears

Special Day

As I dress this dark cold morning,
My thoughts are on this day.
Because today we honor veterans,
Who sacrificed in so many ways.

I put on a shirt of white today,
With emblems of my Corps.
White which stands for purity,
With honor which we served.

Trousers next with stripe of red,
Red for blood our brothers shed.
A cover with emblem of gold,
Eagle globe and anchor bold.

As I dress on this dark cold morn,
My thoughts are of those we mourn.
But also of my family with me now,
Brothers and sisters who share a vow.

As the sun rises to its post today,
I join with my brothers on our way.
To the monuments reminding us,
Of why this is such a special day.

But For The Grace Of God

But for the grace of god any could be me,
A story shared by many others like me.
My clothes are worn and tattered now,
But no one notices or sees me anyhow.

I suffer here alone on the cold, cold street.
But many others like me share this fate.
At one time we all stood proud and tall,
Serving our country but so many would fall.

Now on hard times we are forgotten by all,
A Country cares for others, for us not at all.
For our sacrifice there were promises made,
Now suffering and broken there's nowhere to turn.

Love

of

Family &

Holidays

Family and Friends

So this is Christmas it's finally here,
The hustle is over celebration is near.
Santa has come the gifts are all here,
Time to gather in friendship and cheer.

Some will be happy and some sad,
I will be mindful of what I have had.
Some family I'll see others I won't,
Friends are loved added to the count.

One special friend is absent from here,
I miss them love them color them dear.
I accept the absence as necessity here,
I hope for the future and keep busy here.

At the end of the day satisfaction will reign,
And this Christmas Day will be gone again.
The only thing remaining is family and friends,
The most important ingredient of the day's end

Merry Christmas Marines

On a mountain with no name in a far off land,
A patrol of Marines travel swiftly across the sand.
They camped there together alone on the sand,
With caution and diligence alert hand in hand.

No fire to warm them nor hot food to eat,
Only light from the stars to allow them to see.
This is a special night for the rest of the world,
It's Christmas tonight a time of joy in the world.

We celebrate with family gifts and lights too,
Our Marines have no family to love and cling too.
Even gifts and lights are things way too grand,
Tonight they have each other but no other plan.

The one thing in common we share together,
We both view the stars that span the heavens.
This connection between us though slim it be,
Has to be enough until united we can be.

We in our homes together family and friends,
Miss our Marines especially our friends.
Our message we send out across the stars,
Merry Christmas Marines, Semper Fi to the Corps.

As We Gather Round The Table

As we gather round the table,
To celebrate with family and friends.
I cannot help but remember,
Those departed or missing friends.

There are those who left for heaven,
and dine at a table with the lord.
But others serve around the world,
In places where the table is the floor.

The lands are cruel and hostile,
And they risk their lives each day.
But today is all about our family,
And there's are thousands of miles away.

So they gather there together,
Brothers and sisters one and all.
And share a meal from plastic bags,
On their table on the floor.

So as you slice your turkey,
And you lift your glass of wine.
Remember those who serve us all,
At the risk of precious lives.

The Night Before Christmas

It's Christmas Eve throughout the land, the miracle has begun,
Together waiting hand in hand, the arrival of the new born Son.
The air is crisp, the sky is clear save one bright star to guide us,
It matters not how far we come, but the love we hold inside us.

We asked him for so many things, how can he possibly grant them?
To ease the suffering and cure disease seems impossible to be granted.
Yet hope exists in all our hearts, that all we ask be granted,
Because Christmas is the only time when miracles, are granted.

We ask he gives us peace on Earth, a gift that we will surely cherish,
Imagine if because of this, not a single veteran would perish.
All these gifts we ask of him are not for selfish reasons,
We cherish these, passing them on, to a world better than we found it.

So as I fall asleep tonight with hopes and dreams abounding,
I plan on waking Christmas Day to the gifts that will astound you.
And as I feast on Christmas Day I remember those departed,
Who celebrate this miraculous day in heaven where it started.

Dear Santa

There comes a time in all our lives,
When we grow up and look at life.
And as I sit and start to write,
My list for Santa's Christmas ride.

Dear Santa I would ask from you,
A list of gifts that may seem new.
We have troops in foreign lands,
Watch over them hear their prayers.

Then I ask you for a cure for cancer,
Poverty and homelessness and more.
Then for all my friends far and near,
For family so close to me and dear.

To all my brothers from the Corps,
And the Corps sisters even more.
Happiness and joy may be theirs,
A Merry Christmas for them and theirs.

Tis The Season

It is the season of miracles and joy,
The tree is up and under it the toys.
The house is decorated all around,
And on it colored lights surround.

Before you say that you're all done,
Look around and see what's undone.
Look beyond you yard and fence,
And see the streets, alley and vents.

Behold the faces of the homeless vets,
They lie upon the streets distressed.
Forgotten by the country they served,
Remembered not by you and I.

Don't look away look into there eyes,
You can recognize a glint of pride.
Affected by what was too much to bear,
They suffer in the land which still is theirs

Remember them this time of year,
Before you begin your happy cheer.
The vet whose eyes, you saw the pride,
Should be treated lovingly and kind.

I can't tell you how to accomplish this,
Only that you must try and persist.
Bring them warmth, a coat and gloves,
Or a decent meal that warms there soul.

Whatever you decide only you will know,
But please don't turn your back and go.
It will take much more than you and I,
But with two or more, we build and strive.

The Spirit Of Christmas

You can feel the spirit of Christmas today,
After all, there are only a very few short days.
The trees are all up, the houses are aglow,
Shopping doesn't slow, for even the snow.

Soon we will gather to share in great joys,
As children dive in, to get at their toys.
Adults hoist their glasses in Holiday Cheer,
A feast lies before them meticulously prepared.

As you gather remember, not everyone is at home,
Thousands are in lands both barren and alone.
They gather in the cold, resting in the sand.
Their Holiday Feast comes in brown Plastic bags.

But just as we here, they hold hands and say grace,
Celebrating together in this cold barren place.
They endure it all, no matter how hard,
Their spirit undaunted it's their duty, their job.

I have so many wishes for them this time of year,
Of course coming home for the Holiday Cheer.
Not being possible I pray to the Lord,
God keep them safely, while they serve us abroad.

Maybe each home, besides saying a prayer,
Could place at the table one empty chair.
It won't displace any guest, nor need extra food,
Unless the Miracle of Christmas should break the rules.

On Christmas Eve

On Christmas Eve in a land far away,
A squad of Marines in shifting sands lay.
There's no Christmas star to guide them,
There's no stockings hung with care.

The only semblance of Christmas is,
The freezing cold wind in the air.
As we sit down to dinner family and friends,
I can't help but think of them eating in tins.

We gather in churches to celebrate mass,
As our brothers are out there freezing their ass.
As I kneel in Gods building I humbly pray,
Please help my brothers out of harms way.

Send your breath down to warm them,
And keep watch over them as they sleep.
If you're speaking to Santa there's one gift I seek,
May the spirit of Christmas give each Marine peace.

The Season To Be Jolly

They say it is the season to be jolly,
We shop and sing and hang the holly.
We shop till we drop for what we need not,
Forgetting to be thankful for what we've got.

The stockings are hung with great care,
The trees lights are a big glowing glare.
The presents are wrapped with flare,
Placed beneath the great tree with care.

The family is sleeping tight in their beds,
Dreaming of the festivities which lie ahead.
But some will be missing what lies ahead,
As they fight far away in lands that we dread.

Having no warm blankets or soft beds to sleep,
Only each of their brothers their safety to keep.
No tree with lights glaring, no presents beneath,
No home cooked food spread out as a feast.

So before you sit down to your Christmas feast,
Before opening the presents beneath the tree.
Take a moment to remember a moment to pray,
For all the heroes whose duties keep them away.

Love

of

Nature

Autumn Leaves

The leaves have fallen and coat the ground,
Orange, red, green, yellow and brown.
A vision of beauty for autumns debut,
A show worth seeing by old and new.

The curtain has risen the play has begun,
Natures the author and second to none.
The play is a brief one so be quick to view,
If you dawdle you'll miss it as winter will come.

Children will play there and lovers will walk,
This time is for outdoors before winter balks.
Celebrate this beauty and enjoy the play,
You and your lover will enjoy every day.

The Storm

The storm has passed the sun shines bright,
The wind is blowing leaves both left and right.
They dance and twirl and seem to take flight,
This display of natures is a spectacular sight.

The trees standing tall do bend and sway,
Some still with leaves which cling to stay.
Others leaves that have not yet turned,
The sights around me cause me to turn.

I turn and turn looking up and then down,
The dizziness I feel almost brings me down.
The beauty I behold surpasses all expectations,
The only thing missing is another partaking.

Angel's Weep

Snowflakes fall upon the ground,
Accumulating in little mounds.
Each flake unique in shape and size,
Falling frozen tears from angels eyes.

Angels weep for what they've seen,
Two lovers cast out from their dream.
Left to life's sadness and lonely days,
Quite different from the days we played.

Fate has thrown them an awful curve,
Not what these lovers truly deserve.
So snowflakes fall from crying eyes,
And travel from the heavens high.

They pile upon the ground so high,
How much can angels really cry?
If heavens host can care this much,
Our love is really worth as much.

Surprise

There comes a day in all our lives,
When we awake to a big surprise.
Someone came to us in the dark,
We awoke as someone old and stark.

We gain some weight and slow down,
But still we remain that boyish clown.
The body has aged the mind not so,
It's like something is pulling us to and fro.

You look in the mirror and to your surprise,
Looking back at you is a different guy.
Hair is gray and your eyes seem cold,
You were once so bold and now you're old.

You are in shock your world has changed,
Your body turned old yet you haven't changed.
You feel cheated by life of what could be,
I am so very thankful this never happened to me.

Trails End

A clearing on a trail so still,
A fire smolders warm and still.
A welcome at a cold trails end,
I sit in silence awaiting rides end.

The leaves have fallen but lie still,
There is no wind but a quite a chill.
I hear voices coming from the trail,
It won't be long till end of trail.

Emerging through the naked trees,
Riders high on their mighty steeds.
One by one they majestically stride,
Returning their riders full of pride.

Perhaps life may have gone awry,
Choosing to put these kings aside.
Those who ride these mighty steeds,
Still appreciate their mighty deeds.

Fall

The leaves have turned and begun to fall,
The autumn season takes a heavy toll.
Autumn is the season where all is old,
Next is winter where death takes its toll.

The trees are bare and branches brittle,
Soon snow will fall and freeze with drizzle.
The animals sleep awaiting springtime,
Winters long death is silent and deep.

We long for springtime and chance of birth,
We search as the snow melts for tiny buds.
The cycle of life has begun once again,
Life will bloom plentiful till autumns end.

Distance

Novembers winds are in the air,
This weeks warm, nice and fair.
soon cold and gloom will appear,
And loneliness will fill the air

Winter keeps us inside a lot,
When alone you'd rather not
Too much time to think is bad,
Things remembered seem so sad.

There is one easy answer to my plight,
It's something I used earlier in my life.
The weathers here and everywhere,
I share it here and with you there.

Birth and Renewal

The leaves have filled the trees again,
As soft summer breezes come again.
Seeds give birth to flowers that bloom,
As lovers embrace beneath the moon.

The moon shines brightly across the sky,
And you can see Jupiter close nearby.
Stars and constellations complete the scene,
As lovers lie below in awe of Gods theme.

This is the season of birth and renewal,
Nature as well as lovers come into bloom.
I would love to be alive here with my love,
Holding and kissing beneath the heavens above.

"Darkness cannot drive out darkness only light can do that. Hate cannot drive out hate only Love can do that"

Martin Luther King Jr.

I am a Marine, and an Active member of The Marine Corps League. In my spare time I write Poetry. I am A Graduate of Central Connecticut State University, with an MA in Literature. I live in Prospect Connecticut with my wife Teri.

In this book I have focused on the many aspects of Love. It's easy to fall into the idea that love is about cards and flowers. About walks on the beach and holding hands but Love encompasses so much more than that. We find Love in so many parts of our life and sometimes we fail to realize that. In this work I try to refocus on the Love we miss or take for granted.

www.ingramcontent.com/pod-product-compliance
Ingram Content Group UK Ltd.
Pitfield, Milton Keynes, MK11 3LW, UK
UKHW021655190726
13853UKWH00001B/280

9 798201 618261